THE FEARS AND DREAMS OF EVERLASTING LIFE

A COLLECTION OF DARK POETRY

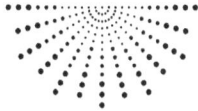

RANDY SPEEG

S B
SASGORA BOOKS

The Fears and Dreams
of Everlasting Life

For my good friend and fellow author Michelle Brumley, who has given me the inspiration and the push to return to writing, and to unearth and publish my old writings. Without her the words contained within would have remained buried in a shallow grave for many more years. She is also one hell of a Demon Slayer, but that's a story for another time. Thank you Michelle.

—Randy Speeg, September 2015

BOOK ONE: A VAMPIRE'S TEARS

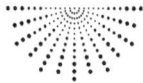

I had seen my becoming a vampire in two lights: The first light was simply enchantment... But the other light was my wish for self-destruction.

—Anne Rice, Interview with the Vampire

Tonight

~

Tonight I stood,
I stood out in the open night,
Felt the wind blow against me,
Looked up into the sky,
Saw only black, white, and lights,
Felt small as branches whipped wildly.

Tonight I spoke,
I spoke and thought about extraordinary
    things,
Spoke of space, planets, and stars,
Thought of death and life and things in
    between,
Told of dreams, visions, and fears,
Talked of things that haunt the soul.

Tonight I listened,
I listened to wind against leaves,
Heard the Heavens' silence,
Listened to the sounds of Earth,
Heard the words of fellow man,
Listened to my voice, mind, and soul.

Tonight I found,
I found answers to questions,

Found new questions to ask,
Discovered new thoughts and ideas,
Found new meaning in a once dull world,
Tonight I found the meaning of life.

Tonight I became a Vampire.

A Vampire's Tears

~

Walking through the weeds
Stepping on the thorns
Of the black roses
Sucking up the pain rain
Falling from my eyes,

Living off the blood
Of a long lost lover
I went in search
And found another
One just as sweet as her,

Drinking your blood I feel the power
Please just stay alive another hour
I want to taste every last drop of you
While I still see human behind your eyes
    of blue,

You give me life
You're not just my lover
I'll suck you dry
So I can have another,

Night without fears
On this carousel of tears.

Tear Open the Dark

I tear open the Dark
And tarnish my flesh,

May thy Light free my soul
From the night's gentle wings,

I beg for the sweet pain
To release my eternal tears,

Welcome, my beautiful death
A thousand years too late,

Dust returns to dust
And Light erases Dark,

The bloodline is severed
And I will be the last.

Plucked

~

Plucked,

From the light of death
To live forever within
The darkness of life,

A rose withers and wilts
In the unobstructed sun
Forced to embrace the night,

Among the lonely flowers
The rose will never die
Or rise to become a butterfly.

The Becoming

~

Staring into those glowing eyes
He freezes,

The fangs digging into his neck
He trembles,

As she slits her wrist
He is dying,

Drinking from her
His body dies,

He drinks and drinks
To his new found life.

Ecstasy Ends

Ecstasy ends and the euphoria
Shudders over my body,

I lay there questioning the truths
Of my own reality,

As my love dies beside me.

Scars

~

Jagged scars of passion
Rest upon my cheeks,

Feverous blood flows into
Tears of pain and joy,

I raise my tongue to her lips
And lick the sweet nectar,

Ambrosia has not a better taste
As she sleeps upon a bed
Of blood & roses.

Embraced

~

You may say that
You've experienced life
But, you have not,

Not until your eyes glow
With an unearthly passion
And your body trembles
With ungodly hunger
Have you lived,

Not until you have died
And your heart has ceased to beat,

Not until your life force
Has been embraced
And that of another
Drips from your lips
Will you know,

Not until emotions
Run through your soul
So strong that you cry
Tears of blood
And the night is your salvation,

Will you have any idea

What it is to be free
And to have lived,

Step into the night
Never to walk in a dead life
Bathed in sunlight again,

Step into the night
And embrace the death
That will bring you eternal life.

Death Becomes You

~

Death Becomes You,
You wear darkness elegantly
Like a silken cloak of pitch black,

Death Becomes You,
When the Moon illuminates
The lustful hunger of your eyes,

Death Becomes You,
As your feral claws
Tear open my warm flesh,

Death Became You,
And now,

Death Becomes Me.

Dark Caress

~

Emerald hues
Behind golden locks
Sanguine lips
Around glistened cocks,

Seduction
Primitive and bold
Abduction
Brutal and cold,

She makes love to her prey
Makes her lovers pray,

Brings pleasure to them all
Right before they fall,

Victims of her sex
Fangs slicing necks,

Tearing open sensual flesh
Blood stained dark caress.

Burning

~

Spiral, spiral, burning bright
Eyes that mar, Eyes that bite,

Hot waves gnashing cold flesh
Cells bursting, Rupture, fluids mesh,

Trembles, quakes, body aches
Shivers, quivers, the sun delivers,

Bursting, popping,
Bubble-wrap skin
The flames distilling
Every ounce of sin,

Falling down, crumbling to ash
Eternity ends in a brutal flash.

Twitching in Twilight

~

Remember when I found you?
Crouched in the alley
Behind that club,

Strung out on Ecstasy
And Moon Beam
You trembled as my shadow
Crossed your face,

I remember the look in your eyes
Two glass orbs
Trapped in my darkness,

Innocence scared to die
Even more frightened
To live,

I knelt beside your soaked body
And took your hand
You eased your fears a bit
Despite the coldness of my skin,

I pulled you close to taste you
And grew hungry from
Your warmth and fear,

I fed on your body and soul
And gave you a drop of my curse,

Frightened of life
Scared of death
And now cursed to both
Forever,

Then I marveled at
Your beautiful desperation
As I left you addicted and
Twitching in twilight.

Jaded Angel

~

Jaded Angel
Walking in desolation
On a plain of stars,

Ten thousand tiny shards
Of broken dreams
Tearing jagged scars,

Killing the hurt with pain
Turning the tears to rain,

Warm, bloody, salty rains
Drop, drop, dropping on the plains,

Of the hard dry earth
Soaking into the cracks
Bringing out life and birth.

BOOK TWO: A WRAITH'S PASSION

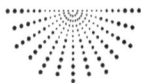

Monsters are real, ghosts are real too. They live inside us, and sometimes, they win.

—Stephen King

A Wraith's Passion

~

Trapped in life
By a dark angel's heart
Obsessive love
Grown from childlike need
Innocence fed
By the darkest lusts,

Forever turned to the dark path
A lover's betrayal cut too deep
Soul longing for escape from pain,

Blade of dark blood pushing through
The reaping of a dark dream
Agony of an eternity never passing,

Until a fatal thought and memory
Clawing through the tempest
Into a rebirth
Becoming an echo of a former self,

Trapped in death
By a dark angel's soul
Dark passion
Grown from obsessive love
Malevolence fed
By lustful fetters,

Wraith haunting
From beyond the shroud
In pursuit of an undying passion
Walking on the edge of
A beautiful Oblivion.

Upon Crimson Wings

~

They came upon crimson wings
Like nightmares demons dream,

They tore through the men
With razor cut claws,

Slashing flesh to ribbons
Trimming victory skins,

They feasted on the young
With poison tipped fangs,

Forked tongues greedily lapping
At marrow milk,

They raped the women
'Til they came sweet red,

Leaving them trembling
In congealed crimson ecstasy.

Empty Bottle

~

Empty is the bottle
Sitting on the table
Reflecting light,

Little people
Running around my head
Chasing skulls,

Small creature
Standing on the ceiling
With a foul gesture,

Twisted is the path
He points to with his finger
Bleeding down on my head,

Long hall, bright light,
That way I cannot go,

Long hall, darkness,
This path I must follow,

Sickness beckons, my faith is gone,
The small creature leads me on.

Sheol

~

Dark black,
Don't see your hand,
Free falling,
Eternal plunge,
Unite in passing,
Fume of smoke,
Irks the senses,
Butterflies squirm,
Mocking voices,
Taunt your indiscretions,
Jeering laughs,
Of you they make fun,
Insulting profanity,
Entertains you,
For the rest of forever.

Ashes to Ashes

~

Ashes to ashes
Gave no comfort
As she lowered,

Dust to dust
Had no meaning
As I wept,

My gift of life
Had betrayed her
In death,

Flesh is flesh
Never to recycle
Into any ash,

Body is soul
Never to transcend
Into any dust.

Wicked Weeds

~

You're a fatal disease
You grow through my heart
Like wicked weeds,

You're a basket case
And I'm trapped between
You're wicker weaves,

You're a killer Queen
And I'm just another drone
In your honeycombed cell,

You're gold digging gravedigger
And now I'm six feet away
From your tomb-stoned Hell.

Limbo Hourglass

Sinking through
The quick sands of time
We have lost our destination,

Forever wondering
If we can ever dig ourselves out
Of this Limbo Hourglass,

Where neither minutes
Nor days have any meaning,

Where death and life
Are one in the same thing,

As we clear the narrow middle
The vassal flips
Trapping us in a continuous cycle,

As seconds become hours
And days and years,

We long for our existence
To have substance again.

Blood Ran Dry

~

Crying for an internal pain
Caused by you,

Choking on your darkness
With every thought of you,

It's all I can do
To just breathe anymore,

And I keep thinking good bye
Good bye you sick thing,

Enough with the torture
And enough with the pain,

Stop eating out my heart
With the sound of your name,

And more tears flow
The bitter saltiness,

And I want you
To know their taste,

To feel your tongue
Slide up my cheek,

To know the texture
Of your thick pink lips,

And I want to be
In your darkness,

Let me be
Your toy for pain,

I can't let you go
So what can I do?

I will write for you
Page after agonizing page,

I'll tell you everything
About little sick me,

The story of my soul
Through the art of words,

To tell you
Everything I know,

To show you
Everything I feel,

To make you understand
My undying desire for you,

So I'll just write and write

And then write some more,

There's so much in me
My heart will pour,

And then you'll see
And then you'll know,

And if you don't
Well...

I'll just write forever
Until my ink runs dry,

And then...

I'll just find a feather
And prick my finger,

And I'll write my love
In my own blood,

And as I cry
And as I die,

You will know
That I loved you,

Until my blood ran dry.

Sick Thing

~

I love you
You sick thing,

The way you think
Those perverted thoughts
That slither through your mind,

The way you speak
Those dirty words
That roll off your tongue,

The way you hurt
The pain you cause
By torturing my soul,

You push me to my limits
You want me to break,

But I cry then laugh
And each time I shake,

I come back for more
Like a sick junkie whore,

I have a twisted desire
To be hurt by you,

I need to be suffocated
By your darkness,

I want to drown
In your tears,

I long to choke
On your desire,

And my skin begs
For the sting of your whip,

I must be incurably insane
To want to share in your pain,

I would die a thousand deaths
To live one life with you,

I love you
You sick thing.

Nightmares

~

Nightmares,
Falling from the skies
Evil gleaming in their eyes,

Nightmares,
Slicing through the air
Killing here and there,

Nightmares,
Shifting in and out
Making people shout,

Nightmares,
Clawing at your brain
Driving you insane.

The Anatomy of Art

~

I slice around curves and edges
Paper cutting savage pulp,

Mâchéing machete ribbons
Plucking and pasting,

Gluing pieces of parts
And parts of hearts,

Sewing a fleshy patchwork
With needle and nerves,

Pipe cleaner arteries
And spider web veins,

Making final touches
With surgical care,

Finger painting the delicate parts
With crimson blush.

Cursed

Trying hard to hate you
To completely forget you
To never ever want you,

But you've made it so damn hard
You're under my skin
And in my veins
Causing such delightful irritation,

I can't scratch you out
For fear of bleeding to death,

But keeping you near
Will surely kill me anyhow,

You're a wicked curse
I've placed upon myself,

And I don't even know
If I want to be free,

Because sometimes there are
Worse things than suffering.

Separated Souls

I cut and cut but
no number of scars will
ever change the line of life
nor the line of the heart
permanently etched into the
palm of my skin,

I bleed and bleed but
the gushing pints will
not empty my heart
any further,

How do you empty a broken vessel?

I stitch and stitch but
the pieces will not mend,

No thread will ever
piece together
Separated Souls.

AFTERWORD

Thank you for taking the time to read my poetry collection. I hope that you enjoyed reading it as much as I enjoyed writing it. I have only one request; if you did like it, please leave a review. Reviews are the lifeblood of indie authors and greatly help us get more books in front of more readers. If you didn't like it, that's fine too, just leave an honest review, that's all I ask.

ABOUT THE AUTHOR

Randy Speeg is a horror, supernatural, and science-fiction writer from Cincinnati, OH. When he's not writing he is an active Libertarian, and also a Union President at his day job. He has been known to moonlight, on occasion, as a paranormal investigator. Randy is currently working on his first novel.

www.RandySpeegAuthor.com

ALSO BY RANDY SPEEG

The Night Has Teeth